THE DEN

The dino den is the friends' favourite place to hang out and practise their hobbies. Can you spot Mazu testing a science experiment and Rocky trying out his new relaxation station?

ZZZZZZ

Can you find:

Caterpillar   Paint & paintbrush   Dragonfly picture   Peach   Gigantopedia

Spyglass

Blue flower

Rock painting

Bone

Gigantosaurus

THE CAVE PLAYGROUND

Shhh – the cave playground is the best kept secret in Cretacia. Come and join us, it's so much fun! Who's that whooshing down the slide?

Can you find:

Arthropleura

Zak

Tori

Rolo

Leena

Plink

Plonk

Plunk

Pineapple

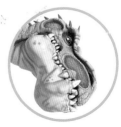

Gigantosaurus

THE FROZEN LANDS

There are lots of snowy mountains and sparkling ice in the Frozen Lands. It's the perfect place for the dinos to have an EPIC snowball fight!

Can you find:

Nest

Rugo

Tori

Rolo

Zak

Dilo Magnifying glass Totor Rocky Gigantosaurus

THE DESERT ARCHES

Ready! Set! Go! It's always fun to race under the desert arches. Can you guess who will ZOOM to the finish line first?

Can you find:

Diplocaulus

Berry

Rugo

Iggy

Rolo

Leena

Cactus   Scorpion   Pterodactyl   Racing flag   Gigantosaurus

THE JUNGLE

The green and leafy jungle hides the most delicious snacks a dino can find – and these dinos are ready for a picnic! Which tasty snack would you choose?

Can you find:

Dragonfly

Pineapple

Jug

Leena

Tori

Rolo

arnivorous plant   Orange flower   Zak   Cror   Totor   Gigantosaurus

THE BEACH

On the beach, you'll find the dinos and their friends playing in the sunshine. But Termy thinks it should be HER beach – watch out for her snapping jaws!

Can you find:

Strange fish

Rock painting

Coconuts

Rugo

Patchy

Marshall

Berry

Scorpion

Bill

Red flower

Gigantosaurus

UNDER THE LAKE

Underwater there's even more to explore. Luckily Bill's Bubble means they can glide through the water like fish! Dive down and take a look around.

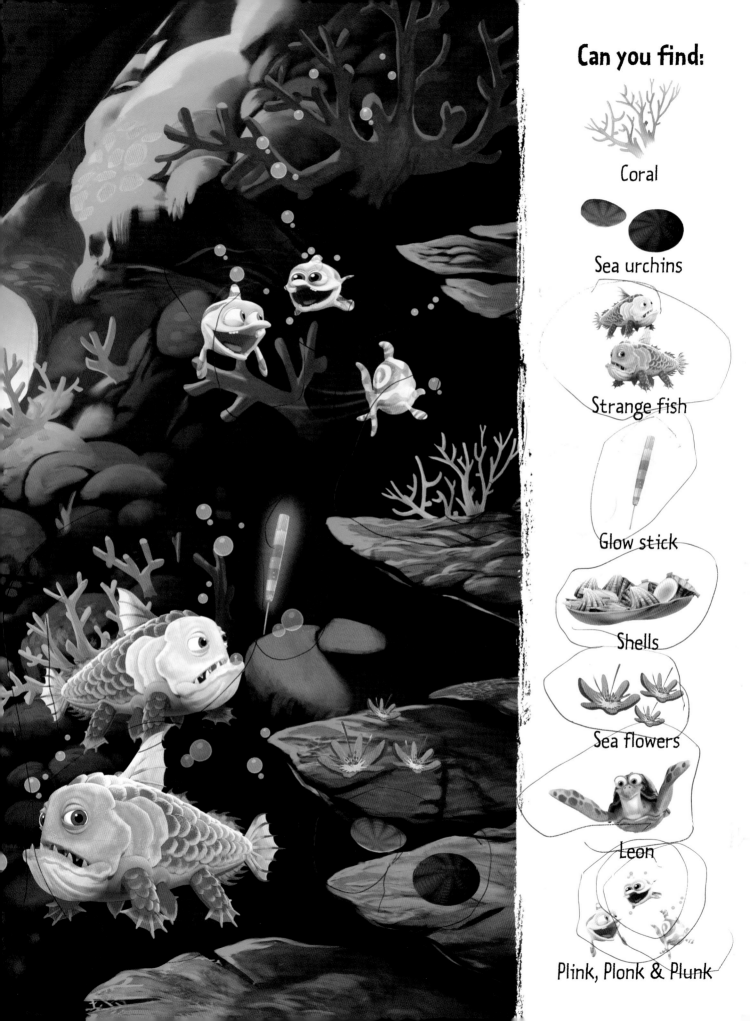

Can you find:

Coral

Sea urchins

Strange fish

Glow stick

Shells

Sea flowers

Leon

Plink, Plonk & Plunk

THE SWAMP

Down by the swamp, it's not safe for little dinos. They use the jetpacks to stay away from the quicksand! But for some, it's the perfect place to have a snack...

Can you find:

Dragonfly

Banana skin

Carnivorous plant

Peach

Orange flower

Archie　　Mazu　　Rugo　　Arthropleura　　Pink flower　　Gigantosaurus

Can you find:

Map

Signpost

Pink flower

Zak   Tori

Berry

Nest

Mushroom

Gigantosaurus

THE WALNUT TREES

You will often find Giganto and Rugo at the walnut trees, tucking into tasty walnuts and big bones. Even though they're Giganto's favourite, he doesn't mind sharing!

Can you find:

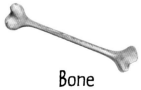

Bone

Arthropleura

Zak

Caterpillar

Rugo

Rock painting

Leena

Rolo

T

Mushroom

Gigantosaurus

THE CREEPY CAVE

When the four dino friends are feeling brave, they venture into the darkest cave in Cretacia – BOO! Here they need LOTS of shiny glow weeds to guide the way.

Can you find:

Purple flower

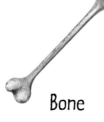

Bone

Diplocaulus

T

Cror

Caterpillar

Scorpion

Dilo

Shiny flower

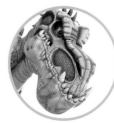

Gigantosaurus

Can you find:

Cactus

Hegan

Patchy

Mazu

Purple flower

THE HOT SPRINGS

What could be better after a busy day in Cretacia than a soak in the hot springs? A soak in the hot springs while hanging out with all your dino friends!

Dragonfly

Iggy

Spinosaurus

Rock painting

Arthropleura

Gigantosaurus

ANSWERS

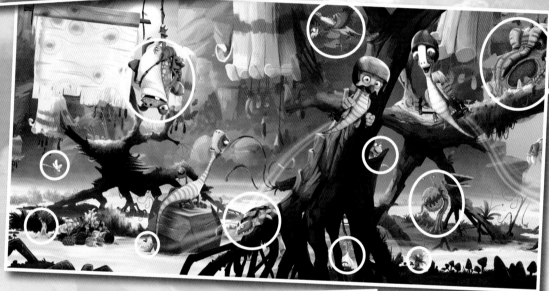

A TEMPLAR BOOK

This book is based on the TV series Gigantosaurus™.
The TV series Gigantosaurus™ is created and produced by Cyber Group Studios.
Based on the original characters created by Jonny Duddle in the book *Gigantosaurus*,
first published by Templar Books in 2014.

First published in the UK in 2024 by Templar Books,
an imprint of Bonnier Books UK
4th Floor, Victoria House,
Bloomsbury Square, London WC1B 4DA
Owned by Bonnier Books
Sveavägen 56, Stockholm, Sweden
www.bonnierbooks.co.uk
Copyright © 2024 by Cyber Group Studios
10 9 8 7 6 5 4 3 2 1
All rights reserved
ISBN 978-1-80078-842-8

Written and edited by Amelia Warren
Designed by Wendy Bartlet
Production by Hannah Cartwright

Printed in China